Christopher Columbus

Letter of Christopher Columbus to Rafael Sanchez

Written on board the caravel while returning from his first voyage

Christopher Columbus

Letter of Christopher Columbus to Rafael Sanchez
Written on board the caravel while returning from his first voyage

ISBN/EAN: 9783337103576

Printed in Europe, USA, Canada, Australia, Japan

Cover: Foto ©ninafisch / pixelio.de

More available books at **www.hansebooks.com**

FACSIMILE

OF

THE FIRST PUBLICATION CONCERNING AMERICA.

———•———

LETTER

OF

Christopher Columbus

TO

RAFAEL SANCHEZ,

WRITTEN ON BOARD THE CARAVEL WHILE RETURNING FROM
HIS FIRST VOYAGE.

PUBLISHED AT BARCELONA, MAY, 1493.

CHICAGO:
THE W. H. LOWDERMILK CO.
1893.

Regnũ hyspanie.

Oceanica Classis

De Jnſulis inuentis

Epiſtola Criſtoferi Colom (cui etas noſtra
multũ debet : de Jnſulis in mari Jndico nup
inuẽtis. Ad quas perquirendas octauo antea
menſe: auſpiciis et ere Jnuictiſſimi Fernandi
Hiſpaniarum Regis miſſus fuerat) ad Mag-
nificum dñm Raphaelez Sanxis: eiuſdẽ ſere-
niſſimi Regis Theſaurariũ miſſa. quam nobi
lis ac litterat⁹ vir Aliander d Coſco: ab Hiſ-
pano ydeomate in latinũ conuertit: tercio kł's
Maij. M.cccc.xciij. Pontificatus Alexandri
Sexti Anno Primo.

Qoniam ſuſcepte prouintie rem p-
fectam me pſecutum fuiſſe: gratũ ti
bi foze ſcio: has pſtitui cxarare: que
te vniuſcuiuſcꝗ rei in hoc noſtro iti-
nere geſte inuenteꝗ admoneát. Triceſimoter
tio die poſt ꝗ Gadibus diſceſſi: in mare Jndi-
cũ perueni: vbi plurimas Jnſulas innumeris
habitatas hominib⁹ repperi: quaꝝ oim p feli-
ciſſimo Rege noſtro: preconio celebzato ꝝ ve-
xillis extenſis: cõtradicente nemine poſſeſſio-
nẽ accepi. primeꝗ earum: diui Saluatoris no
men impoſui (cuius fret⁹ auxilio) tam ad hãc
ꝗ ad ceteras alias puenim⁹. Eam vero Jndi

j

Insula hyspana

Guanabanyn vocant.Aliaʒ etiã vnã quanᷓ
nouo nomine nuncupaui.Quippe aliam Jnſu
lam Sancte Marie Cõceptiõis.aliam Fernã⸗
dinam.aliaʒ ħyſabellam.aliã Jobanam.ꝛ ſic
de reliquis aꝑpellari iuſſi.Quãpꝛimũ i eã Jn⸗
ſulam quã dudũ Jobanam vocari dixi aꝑpuli
mus:iuxta ei⁹ littus occidentẽ verſus aliquã⸗
tulum pꝛoceſſi:tamᷓ eam magnã nullo reper
to fine inueni:vt non inſulam:ſed cõtinentem
Chataʸ pꝛouinciã eſſe crediderim:nulla tamẽ
videˢ opꝑida municipiaue in maritimis ſita cõ
finibus:pꝛeter aliquos vicosꝛpꝛedia ruſtica:
cum quoꝛũ incolis loqui nequibam:quare ſi⸗
mul ac nos videbant ſurripiebãt fugam.Pꝛo
grediebar vltra:exiſtimans aliquam me vꝛbẽ
villaſue inuenturum.Deniᷓ videns ᵱ longe
admodum ᵱgreſſis:nibil noui emergebat:et
huiuſmodi via nos ad Septentrionem defere
bat:ᵱipſe fugeꝛe exoptabam:terris etenim re
gnabat bꝛuma:ad auſtrumᷓ erat in voto cõ⸗
tendere:nec minus venti fiagitantibus ſucce⸗
debãt.cõſtitui alios nõ operiri ſucceſſus:et ſic
retrocedens ad poꝛtum quendaʒ quem ſigna⸗
ueram ſum reuerſus:vnde duosħoies ex no⸗
ſtris in terram miſi.qui inueſtigarent:eſſet ne
Rex in ea pꝛouincia/vꝛbeſue alique.ħ̃ii per

ij

Fernadra · hyspana · Jsabella · Saluatorié · Concepoiõ · mercorié

tres dies ambularūt: inuenerūtǧ innumeros
populos z habitatões: paruas tñ et abſǧ vllo
regimine:quaꝓropt redierūt. Jnterea ego iā
intellexerā a ǧbuſdam Jndis:quos ibidē ſu
ſceperā: quõ hmõi ꝓrouincia:inſula quidem
erat.z ſic perrexi oꝛientē verſus:eiꝰ ſemꝑ ſtrin
gens littoꝛa vſǧ ad miliaria .cccxxij. vbi ipſiꝰ
inſule ſunt extremā.hinc aliā inſulā ad oꝛien
tem ꝓroſpexi :oiſtantem ab hac Johana milia
ribus.liiij.quā ꝓrotinus Hiſpanam oixi:in eā
ǧ cõceſſi: z oirexi iter quaſi ꝑ Septentrionez
quēadmodū in Johana ad oꝛientem:miliaria
olxiiij.que oicta Johana z alie ibidem iuſule
ǧfertiliſſime exiſtunt. Hec multis atǧ tutiſſi
mis z lātis:nec alijs quos vnǧ viderim cõpa
randis poꝛtibꝰ: eſt circūdata.multi maximi z
ſalubꝛes hanc interfluūt fluuij.multi quoǧ et
eminētiſſimi in ea ſunt montes. Oñes he inſu
lē ſunt pulcerrime z varijs oiſtincte figuris: ꝑ
uie:z maxima arboꝝ varietate ſidera lamben
tiū plene:ǧs nūǧ folijs ꝓriuari credo : quip
pe vidi eas ita virētes atǧ oecoꝛas: ceu mēſe
Maio i hiſpania ſolēt eē:ǧꝝ alie floꝛētes:alie
fructuoſe:alie i alio ſtatu:ꝓm vniuſcuiuſǧ ǧli
tatē vigebāt:garriebat philomena:z alij paſſe
res varij ac inūmeri:mēſe Nouēbꝛis ǧ ipe per
eas oeambulabā. Sunt ꝓterea in oicta inſula
iij

Iobana septẽ vel octo palmax genera: q̃ pce
ritate z pulchzitudĩe (quẽadmodũ cetere oẽs
arbozes/berbe/fruciuſcꝗ)nfas facile ex̃uperãt
Sũt z mirabiles pin⁹/agri/z pzata vaſtiſſima/
varie aues/varie mella/variacꝗ metalla:ferro
ex̃cepto. Jn ea aũt quã Ỻiſpanã fupza dixim⁹
nũcupari : maxĩmi funt mõtes ac pulcri:vaſta
rura/nemoza/ campi feraciſſimi/ſeri/ pacifcꝗ z
cõdendis edificijs aptiſſimi. Poztuũ in bac in
ſula cõmoditás: z p̃ſtantia fluminũ copia ſalu
bzitate admixta boĩm:q̃ niſi quis viderit: cre
dulitatẽ fupat. Ỻuius arbozes paſcua z fruct⁹
multum áb illis Jobane differũt. Ỻec p̃terea
biſpana diuerſo aromatis genere/ auro/ me
talliſcꝗ abundat. cui⁹ quidẽ z oĩm aliax̃ quas
ego vidi: z quax̃ cognitionẽ babeo:ícole vtri
uſcꝗ fexus nudi ſemp incedũt : quẽadmodum
edunt in lucem. pzeter aliquas feminas. q̃ fo
lio frondeue aliq̃: aut bombicino velo: pudẽ
da operiũt:q̃õ ĩp̃e ſibi ad ld negocij parãt. Ca
rent bi oẽes (vt fupza dixi) quocuncꝗ genere
ferri. carent z armiis: vtpote ſibi ignotis nec ad
ea ſũt apti. nõ ꝓp̃ cozpis defozmitatẽ (cũ ſint
bñ fozmati)ſz qz ſũt timidi ac pleni formidine.
geſtãt tñ ꝓ armiis arũdines ſole puſtas:l quax̃
radicib⁹ baſtile q̃ddã ligneũ ſiccũ z in mucro
nẽ attenuatũ ſigũt:necꝗ bis audẽt iugif vti:nã

Oceanica Classis

sepe euenit cū miserim duos vel tris homines
ex meis ad aliquas villas:vt cū eaʒ loquerē-
tur incolis:exijsse agmē glomeratū ex Indis:
et vbi nostros apropinquare videbāt:fugam
celeriter arripuisse: despʒetis a patre liberis ʒ
ecōtra. ʒ hoc nō ꝙ cuipiam eozū damnū aliꝗs
vel iniuria illata fuerit:immo ad quoscū ꝗs ap
puli ʒ ꝗbus cū verbū facere potui: quicꝗd ha
bebā sum elargitꝰ:pannū aliaꝗ pmulta:nulla
mihi facta versura : sed sunt natura pauidi ac
timidi. Ceteʒ vbi se cernūt tutos:oīi metu re
pulso:sunt ad modū simplices ac bone fidei:ʒ
in oībus que habent liberalissimi:roganti ꝙ
possidet inficiaʒ nemo:quin ipsi nos ad id po-
scendum inuitāt. Maximū erga oēs amorē p-
seferūt:dāt queꝗ magna p paruis. minima lʒ
re nibiloue ꝑtenti:ego attn phibui ne tam mi
nima ʒ nulliꝰ pcij bisce darent:vt sunt lancis/
parapsidū /vitriꝗ fragmēta/jteʒ claui/ligule/
quanꝗ si hoc poterāt adipisci:videbaʒ eis pul
cerrima mūdi possidere iocalia. Accidit enim
quēdam nauitā : tantū auri pondus habuisse
p vna ligula : quāti sūt tres aurei solidi : ʒ sic
alios p alijs miozis pcij:ꝑftim p blanquis no
uis:ʒ ꝗbusdā nūmis aurcis:p ꝗbꝰ habēdis da
bāt qcꝗd petebat vēditoʒ:puta vnciā cū dimi
dia ʒ duas auri:vl trigīta. ʒ ꝗdragīta bombici

pondo:quã ipi iã nouerãt.jtē arcuum/ampho
re/hydrie/oolijcp fragmēta:bombicer auro tã
cp beſtie cõparabãt. qd quia iniquũ ſane erat:
vetui:oedicp eis multa pulcra z grata q̃ mecũ
tulerã nullo iterueniēte p̃mio:vt eos mihi fa=
cill⁹ ɔciliarē:fierētcp r̃picole:z vt ſint pzoni in
amozē erga ʀegēʀeginã principeſcp noſtros
et vniuerſas gētes Hiſpanie:ac ſtudeãt pq̃re=
re z coaceruare:es cp nobis tradere q̃b⁹ip̃i af=
fluũt z noſ magnope ĩdigem⁹. Nullã hij nozũt
ydolatriã:imo firmiſſime credũt oēʒ vim: oēʒ
potētiã:oia denicp bona eſſe ĩ celo: mecp inde
cũ his nauib⁹ z nautiſ oeſcēdiſſe:atʒ B aĩo vbĩ
fui ſuſceptus poſt q̃ metũ repulerãt. Nec ſunt
ſegnes aut rudes:quin ſummi ac p̃ſpicacis in=
genij:z hoĩes qui tranſfretãt mare illõ:nõ ſine
admiratiõe vniuſcuiuſcp rei ratiõe reddunt:
ſed nũ q̃ viderunt gentes veſtitas:necp naues
hmõi. Ego ſtatım atcp ad mare illõ pueni:e pzi
ma inſula quoſdã Jndos violenter arripui: q̃
ediſcerēt a nobis :z nos piter oocerent ea:q̃ p̃
ipſi in hiſce partibus cognitiõe habebant. et
ex voto ſucceſſit:nã breui nos ip̃os:z hij nos:
tum geſtu ac ſignĩs:tum verbis intellexerunt.
magnocp nobis fuere emolumēto. veniunt mõ
mecũ tñ qui ſemp putant me oeſiluiſſe e celo
q̃uis oiu nobiſcũ verſati fuerint hodiecp ver=

senf. τ bi erant primi: q̃ id quocūq̃ appellaba
mus nunciabāt:alÿ ꝺeinceps alÿs elata voce
ꝺicētes. Uenite venite τ videbitis gētes ethe
reas. Quãobzē tã femie q̃ viri: tã impuberes
q̃ adulti:tam iuuenes q̃ senes: ꝺposita formi
ꝺine paulo ante ꝑccpta :nos certatim vifebāt
magna iter ſtipāte caterua alÿs cibū/ alÿs po
tum afferentibꝰ:maxio cū amoze ac beniuolē=
tia incredibili. Habz vnaqueq̃ infula multas
fcaphas folidi ligni:τ fi anguſtas:longitudine
tñ ac forma noſtris biremibꝰ fimiles:curfu aũt
velocioze. Regunf remis tantū modo. Harū
quedã funt magne:quedã parue:quedã i me=
ꝺio ꝑfiſtunt. Plures tamē biremi que remigēt
ꝺu oꝺeuiginti tranſtris maiozes:cū qbꝰ in oēs
illas infulas:que innumere funt:traifcif. cūq̃
his fuã mercaturã exercēt:et inter eos comer=
tia fiunt. Aliquas ego harū biremium feu fca=
pharū:vidi q̃ vehebāt feptuaginta τ octuagin
ta remiges. In omnibꝰ his infulis nulla eſt ꝺi=
uerfitas inter gentis effigies. nulla in mozibus
atq̃ loquela:quin oēs fe intelligūt aduuicē:
que res putilis eſt ad id qō fereniſſimū Regē
noſtrū exoptare precipue reoz:fc̃z eoꝝ ad fan
ctam xp̃i fidem ꝑuerſionē. cui quidē quantum
itelligere potui facilimi funt τ pni. Dixi quē=

admodũ fum pgreffus antea infulã Johanaz
p rectũ tramitez occafus in ozientem miliaria
cccxxij. fm quã viã z intuallũ itineris poffum
dicere hãc Johanã effe maiozẽ Anglia z Scu
tia fil'manqz vltra dicta. cccxxij. paffuũ milia:
in ea pte q̃ ad occidentẽ pfpectat : due : quas
non petij : fup funt puincie: quaz alterã Jndi
Anan vocãt : cui9 accole caudati nafcunt. Zẽ
dunt in longitudinem ad miliaria. clxxx. vt ab
his q̃s vebo mecũ Jndis pcepi: qui omis bas
callẽt iũfulas. Hifpane vero ambit9 maioz eft
tota Hifpania a cologna vfqz ad fontẽ rabidũ
Hincqz facile arguit q̃ quartũ ei9 lat9 qðipe
p rectã lineã occidentis in ozientẽ traieci: mili
aria ptinet. oxl. Hec infula ẽ affectãda z affe-
ctata nõ fpernẽda in qua z fi aliaz olim vt dixi
p inuictiffimo Rege nfo folenniter poffeffio-
nem accepi: earũqz imperiũ dicto Regi peni-
tus cõmittit: i opoztuniozi tñ loco: atqz omi lu
cro z cõmertio pdecenti: cuiufdã magne ville:
cui Natiuitatis dñi nomẽ dedim9: poffeffionẽ
peculiariter accepi. ibiqz arcem quandaz eri-
gere extemplo iuffi: que modo iam debet effe
pãcta: in qua boies qui neceffarij funt vifi: cũ
omi armoz genere: z vltra annũ victu opoztu
no reliq. Jtẽ quãdã carauellã: z p alijs pftruẽ
dis tã i bac arte q̃ in ceteri peritos: ac eiufdẽ

Insula hyspana

insule Regis erga nos beniuolentiã τ familia
ritatẽ incredibilẽ. Sũt eñ gẽtes ille amabiles
admodũ τ benigne: eo ꝙ Rex ꝑdictus me fra
trem suum dici gloꝛiabaf. Et si animũ reuoca
rent: τ his ꝗ i arce manserũt nocere velint: ne
queũt: quia armis carẽt: nudi ĩcedũt: τ nimiũ
timidi. ideo dictã arcem tenẽtes: dũtaxat pñt
totã eã insulã nullo sibi ĩminente discrimine
(dũmodo leges quas dedim²ac regimẽ nõ ex
cedãt) facile detinere. In oñib⁹ his insulis vt
intellexi: quisꝗvni tñ ꝓiugi acquiescit: ꝑter
pꝛincipes aut reges: ꝗbus viginti habere licꜩ.
Femine magis ꝗ̃ viri laboꝛare videnf: nec be
ne potui intelligere an habeãt bona ꝓpꝛia: vi
di eñ ꝗð vn⁹ habebat alijs ĩpartiri: ꝑ̃ptim da
pes/ obsonia/ τ hmõi. Nullũ apð eos monstꝛ
reperi: vt pleriꝗ existimabant: sed hoĩes ma
gne reuerẽtie atꝗ benignos. Nec sunt nigri ve
lut ethiopes. habẽt crines planos ac demissos
nõ degunt vbi radioꝛũ solaris emicat caloꝛ. p
magna nãꝗ hic est solis vehementia: ꝓpterea
ꝙ abeq̇noctiali linea distat. vbi videtur/ gra
dus sex τ viginti Ex montiũ cacuminib⁹ ma
ximũ ꝗ̃ viget frig⁹: sꝫ id ꝗdem moderanf In
di: tũ loci ꝓsuetudie: tũ rex calidissimaꝝ ꝗb⁹
frequẽter τ luxuriose vescunf pꝛesidio. Itaꝗ
mõstra aliꝗ̃ nõ vidi: neꝗ eoꝝ alicubi habui co

gnitionem:excepta quada; infula Charis nů=
cupata : que fecunda ex Hifpana in Indiam
tranffretātibus exiſtit. quam gens quedam a
finitimis habita fcrocioz incolit'. hi carne hu=
mana veſcunf. Habent pzedicti biremiũ gene
ra plurima:quibus in omnes Indicas infulas
traijciunt/depzedāt/furripiũt q; quecũ q; pñt .
Ñibil ab aljs differunt niſ q; gerunt moze fe=
mineo longos crines. vtunf arcub' et fpiculis
arundineis:fixis(vt dixim')in groſſioz pte at
tenuatis haſtilib'.ideo q; habēt feroces:qua=
re céteri Indi inexbauſto metu plectuntur: fz
hos ego nihili facio plus q; alios. Hi ſunt qui
coeunt cum quibuſdam feminis:que ſole infu
lam Mateunin pzimã ex Hifpana in Indiam
traijcientib' habitant.He autē femine nulluz
ſui ſexus opus exercent:vtunf eñ arcub' τ fpi
cuľ ſicuti ð eaz piugib' dixi muniũt: feſe lami
nis eneis q̃z maxia apð eas copia exiſtit .Ali
am mihi infulā affirmant fupzadicta Hifpana
maiozē: ei' incole carēt pilis.auro q; inf alias
potiſſimũ exuberat.Hui' infule τ aliaz q̃s vi
di hoïes mecũ pozto:q̃ hoz q̃ dixi teſtimoniũ
phibēt.Deniq; vt nři difceſſus et celeris reuer
ſióis cōpēdiũ:ac emolumētũ bzeuib' aſtringã
B polliceoz:me nřis Regib' inuictiſſimis puo
eoz fultũ auxilio:tantũ auri datuz quantum

eis fuerit opus.tm̃ vero aromatuz.bombicis.
masticis(q̃ apud Chium dũtaxat inuenit)tan
tũqz ligni aloes.tantum suoz hydrophilato=
rum:quantũ eozũ maieftas voluerit exigere .
jtem reubarbarũ talia aromatuz genera:q̃ bi
quos in dicta arce reliqui iã inuenisse:atqz in=
uenturos existimo.q̃fiquidem ego nullibi ma=
gis fum mozatus nifi quantũ me coegerũt vẽ=
ti:pzeterq̃ in villa Flatiuitatis:dũ arcem con=
dere z tuta omĩa effe pzouidi.Que z fi maxia
et inaudita funt : multo tamẽ maiora fozent fi
naues mihi vt ratio exigit fubuenissent.Uez
multũ ac mirabile hoc:nec noftris meritis coz
refpondẽs:fed fancte Chziftiane fidei:noftro=
rumqz Regũ pietati ac religioni: quia q̃ hu=
manus cõfequi nõ poterat intellectus:id hũa=
nis conceffit diuinus. Solet em̃ deus fuos fu
os:qui qz fua pzecepta diligũt:etiã ĩ impoffibili=
bus exaudire:vt nobis ĩ pñtia ptigit:q̃ ea pfe
cuti fumº:q̃ hactenº mozaliũ vires mĩme atti
gerãt.nã fi haz infulaz q̃piã aliq̃d fcpfeft aut
locuti fũt:oẽs pambages z piecturas nemo fe
eas vidiffe afferit:vĩ ppe videbat fabula Jgi
tur Rex z Regia pncipes ac coz regna felicif
fima: cũcteqz alie Chziftianoz puincie Salua
tozi dño nr̃o Jefu xp̃o agamº gfas:q̃ tãta nos
victozia munereqz donauit:celebzẽt pceffiões

peragant solennia sacra.festacҙ fronde velent
velubra.Exultet Chrift°ī terris:queadmodū
in celis exultat:cum tot populozum pditas añ
hac animas saluatum iri preuidet.Letemur τ
nos:tū ppter exaltationē noftre fidei.tum pp
pter rerū tempozaliū incremēta:quoҙ nō solū
hifpania sed vniuersu Chriftianitas eft futu=
ra pticeps.Hec vt gefta sunt sic breuiter enar=
rata.Uale.Ulifbone pzidie ydus Marcij.

Criftofoz° Colom Oceane clafsis Pzefect°.

Epigrama.R.L.de Cozbaria Epifcopi
Montifpalufij
Ad Inuictifsimū Regē hifpaniaҙ

Jam nulla hifpanis tellus addēda triūphis:
   Atcҙ parum tantis virib°/ozbis erat.
Nunc longe Eois regio depzensa sub yndis.
   Auctura eft titulos Betice magne˙tuos.
Unde repertozi mcrito referenda Colūbo
   Gratia:fҙ summo eft maioz habēda deo:
Qui vincēda parat noua regna tibicҙ fibicҙ:
   Tecҙ simul fortem pzeftat τ efse pium.

Fernãdº rex byspaniaʒ

Granata:

TRANSLATION.

LETTER OF CHRISTOPHER COLUMBUS, the great benefactor of the present age, concerning the newly discovered islands of India upon the Ganges, upon which enterprise he was despatched eight months since by the invincible Sovereigns of Spain, Ferdinand and Isabella; directed to Don Rafael Sanchez, Treasurer of their most Serene Highnesses. Translated from the Spanish into Latin by Leandro de Cosco, April 25, 1493, first year of the pontificate of Alexander VI.

As I know you will take pleasure in hearing of the success of my undertaking, I have determined to send you an account of the occurrences of my voyage and discoveries. Thirty-three days after my departure from Cadiz I arrived in the sea of India, where I discovered many islands, inhabited by innumerable people. Of these I took possession in the name of our fortunate monarch, with public proclamation and colors flying, no one offering any resistance. I named the first of these islands San Salvador, thus bestowing upon it the name of our holy Saviour, under whose protection I made the discovery. The Indians call it Guanahanyn. I gave also a new name to the others, calling the second Santa Maria de la Concepcion, the third Fernandina, the fourth Isabella, the fifth Juana. In the same manner I named the rest. Arriving at the one last mentioned, I sailed along the coast toward the West, discovering so great an extent of land that I could not imagine it to be an island, but the continent of Cathay. I did not, however, discover upon the coast any large cities, all we saw being a few villages and farms, with the inhabitants of which we could not obtain any communication, they all flying at our approach. I continued my course, still expecting to meet with some town or city, but after having gone a great distance, and not meeting with any, and finding myself proceeding toward the North, which I was desirous to avoid on account of the cold, and, moreover, meeting with a contrary wind, I determined to return to the South, and, therefore, put about and sailed back to a harbour which I had before observed.

At this place I sent two men into the country to see if the king or any cities were to be found. These returned in three days, having discovered a great number of towns, but all of them small, and without any government. In the meantime I had learned from certain Indians whom I had taken here that this country was an island. I returned along the coast to the east, a distance of three hundred and twenty-two miles, which brought me to the extremity of the island. Here I discovered to the East another island, fifty-four miles from Juana. I gave it the name of Espanola, and coasted along the island to the North as at Juana I had proceeded to the East, a distance of five hundred and sixty-four miles. All these islands are very fertile. That of Juana abounds in safe and capacious harbours, which surpass in excellence all I have ever seen elsewhere. It is watered by a great number of large and pleasant rivers, and contains many high mountains.

These islands are of a beautiful appearance, and present a great diversity of views. They may be traversed in any part, and are adorned with a great variety of exceedingly lofty trees, which to appearance never lose their foliage, for I saw them as verdant and flourishing as they exist in Spain in the month of May, some covered with flowers, others loaded with fruit, according to their different species and their season of bearing, the whole offering a spectacle of great beauty. The nightingale and countless other birds were singing, although it was the month of November when I visited this delightful region. There are, in the island of Juana, six or eight sorts of palm trees, superior to those of our land in height and beauty, and this superiority is likewise observable in the other trees as well as in the herbs and fruits. Here are to be seen the most beautiful pine trees and the most extensive fields and pastures, a great variety of birds, several sorts of honey, and many kinds of metal, with the exception of iron. In the island named Espanola there are lofty and beautiful mountains, large cultivated tracts, woods, fertile fields, and everything adapted to the purposes of agriculture, the pasturage of cattle, and the erection of houses. The excellence of the harbours here, and the abundance of the streams which contribute to the salubrity of the climate, exceed imagination. There is a considerable di٫ · ference between the trees, fruits, and fields of this island and those of Juana, but here are found divers sorts of precious drugs, gold, and metals. The inhabitants of both sexes, in Espanola, and all the other islands which I saw or heard of, go naked as they were born, all except a few females who wear at the waist a green leaf, a portion of cotton, or bit of silk, which they manufacture for this purpose.

As I before remarked, they possess no iron, and they neither use nor are acquainted with weapons, to the exercise of which indeed they are not at all adapted, not by reason of any corporal deficiency, as they are very well shaped, but on account of their great timidity. Instead of arms they have canes dried in the sun, to the largest ends of which they fix a piece of wood sharpened at the end; of these, however, they have not the courage to make much use. I have in many instances sent two or three of my men to their towns to communicate with the inhabitants, when the Indians would tumultuously rush out, and seeing our people drawing near, run away with such haste that the father would abandon his child and the child his father. This timidity was not owing to any violence or injury we offered them, as I was in the practice of making presents of cloth and other things to all the natives whom I met, but arose from their natural mildness and want of courage. Notwithstanding this, as soon as they have thrown aside their fear, and consider themselves in safety, they are very ingenuous and honest, and display great liberality with whatever they possess.

They never refuse to give any thing away which is demanded of them, and will even themselves entreat an acceptance of their property. They exhibit a great friendship towards every one, and will give whatever they have for a trifle or nothing at all. I forbade my men to purchase any thing of them with such worthless articles as bits of earthenware, fragments of platters, broken glass, nails, and thongs of leather, although when they got possession of any such thing they valued it as highly as the most precious jewel in the world. In this manner of bartering, a sailor has acquired for a leather strap or piece of rope, gold to the amount of three sueldos. Others have obtained as much for a matter of still lower value. For new Spanish coins they would give any thing asked of them, as an ounce and a half or two ounces of gold, or thirty or forty pounds of cotton. Thus they would trade away their cotton and gold like idiots, for broken hoops, platters and glass. I prohibited their traffic on account of its injustice, and made them many presents of useful things which I had carried with me, for the purpose of gaining their affection, in order that they may receive the faith of Jesus Christ, be well disposed towards us, and be inclined to submit to the King and Queen, our Princes, and all the Spaniards, and furthermore that they may furnish us with the commodities which abound among them and we are in want of.

They are not idolators, but believe that all power and goodness is in heaven, and that I had proceeded from that place with my ships and men; under this notion they received me at my first arrival as soon as they had banished their fear. They are not stupid and indolent, but acute and sagacious. Those of them who navigate the seas among those islands give singular accounts of what they have observed upon their voyages, but have never seen people who wear clothes, nor any ships similar to ours. On my arrival I took by force from the first island a few of the Indians, in order that we might become acquainted with one another's language, and to gain a knowledge of what their country contained. These were of singular use to us, as we came to understand each other in a short time by the help of words and signs. I have them still with me, and they continue in the belief that we come from heaven. This information they published wherever we arrived, exclaiming in a loud voice, "Come! come! and see the celestial people." Upon this call, the natives would come thronging to us, after having banished the fear which seized them at first, men, women and children, old and young, crowding the roads and bringing us victuals and drink, with the utmost affection and reverence.

In every one of these islands there are a great number of canoes, each one made of a solid log, of a narrow shape, somewhat resembling our fustas, but swifter in the water; they are navigated solely by oars. They are of different sizes, the most of them containing seats for eighteen rowers. Throughout these islands there is no diversity in the appearance of the people, their manners or language, all the inhabitants understanding one another; a very favorable circumstance, in my opinion, to the design which I have no doubt is entertained by our king, namely, to convert them to the holy Christian faith, to which as far as I can perceive they are well disposed. I have said that I sailed from W. to E. three hundred and twenty-two miles along the island of Juana; from the length of this course I am confident that this island is larger than England and Scotland together, for besides the extent which I coasted there are two other provinces to the West which I did not survey. One of these is named by the Indians Anam, and contains inhabitants with tails. These tracts extend to the distance of a hundred and eighty miles, as I have learnt from the Indians with me, who are well acquainted with them.

The island of Espanola is as large as that part of Spain which extends from Catalonia to Fontarabia, which I infer from the extent of that side of it which I sailed along, being five hundred and forty miles in length. I took possession of this fine island, as I had done of the others, in the name of our invincible king ; and fixed upon a spot for a large city here, as I judged it the most favorable place. I called it Navidad, and ordered the construction of a fortress here, which is by this time finished. At this place I left a sufficient number of men, with all sorts of arms, and a sufficiency of provisions for above a year. I also left them a caravel and expert workmen, after having secured them the friendship of the king of this part of the country. The people are a friendly and amiable race, and the king took a pride in calling himself my brother. Even if their sentiments should change, and they should become hostile towards us, they will not be able to effect any injury to those who remain at the fortress, as they are destitute of weapons, go naked, and are very cowardly, so that those whom I have left there will be able to retain the whole island in subjection without any danger, if they adhere to the regulations with which I charged them.

Each of the natives, as far as I can understand, has one wife, with the exception of the King and Princes, who are permitted to have as many as twenty. The women appear to do more labour than the men. Whether there exists any such thing here as private property I have not been able to ascertain, as I have observed that an individual has been set to distribute to the others, in particular, food and such things. I found no ferocious, sanguinary people in these parts, as some seem to have imagined the people here to be, but they are a very mild and friendly race. Their color is not black like that of the Ethiopians. Their hair is lank and hanging down. They do not inhabit those parts where the sun's rays are very powerful, as the heat is excessive here, the latitude being apparently twenty-six degrees. On the summits of the mountains the cold is great, but they do not suffer any incommodity from it, by being accustomed to the climate, and by the use of hot meats and drinks, which they consume very prodigally.

People of a monstrous description I saw none nor heard of any, except those of the island named Caris, which is the second on the course from Espanola to India; this island is inhabited by people who are regarded by their neighbors as exceedingly ferocious; they feed upon human flesh. These people have many sorts of canoes, with which they make incursions upon all the isles of India, robbing and plundering wherever they go. Their difference from the others consists in their wearing long hair like that of the women, and in using bows and arrows of cane, these last constructed, as I have already related, by fixing a piece of sharpened wood at the larger end. On this account they are deemed very ferocious by the other Indians, and are much feared by them; I think, however, these men are precisely like the others. These are the natives who go to visit the females, who are the sole inhabitants, of the island of Matenin, which is the first on the route from Espanola to India. These women exercise none of the common occupations of their sex, but manage the bow and dart, as we are told of the ancients. They wear armour made of plates of copper, of which metal they have great abundance.

I am assured by the Indians that there is another island, larger than Espanola, whose inhabitants are without hair, and who possess a greater quantity of gold than the others. From this island, as well as the others, I have taken some of the inhabitants to confirm the accounts which I give.

Finally, to sum up the whole, and state briefly the great profits of this voyage, I am enabled to promise the acquisition, by a trifling assistance from their Majesties, of any quantity of gold, drugs, cotton, and mastick, which last article is found only in the island of Scio; also any quantity of aloe, and as many slaves for the service of the marine as their Majesties may stand in need of. The same may be said of rhubarb, and a great variety of other things, which, I have no doubt, will be discovered by those I have left at the fort, as I did not stop long at any single place, unless obliged to do so by the weather, with the exception of the city of Navidad, where we made some stay to build the fort and provide the necessary securities for the place.

Although the discoveries actually accomplished appear great and surprising, yet I should have effected much more had I been furnished with a proper fleet. Nevertheless, the great success of this enterprise is not to be ascribed to my own merits, but to the holy Catholic faith and the piety of our Sovereigns, the Lord often granting to men what they never imagine themselves capable of effecting, as he is accustomed to hear the prayers of his servants and those who love his commandments, even in that which appears impossible; in this manner has it happened to me, who have succeeded in an undertaking never before accomplished by man. For although some persons have written or spoken of the existence of these islands, they have all rested their assertions upon conjecture, no one having ever affirmed that he saw them, on which account their existence has been deemed fabulous.

And now ought the King, Queen, Princes, and all their dominions, as well as the whole of Christendom, to give thanks to our Saviour Jesus Christ, who has granted us such a victory and great success. Let processions be ordered, let solemn festivals be celebrated, let the temples be filled with boughs and flowers. Let Christ rejoice upon earth as he does in heaven, to witness the coming salvation of so many people heretofore given over to perdition. Let us rejoice for the exaltation of our faith, as well as for the augmentation of our temporal prosperity, in which not only Spain, but all Christendom shall participate. Such are the events which I have described to you with brevity. Adieu.

CHRISTOPHER COLUMBUS,
Admiral of the Armada of the Ocean.
LISBON, *March 14th.*